D1321821

Parenting without God:

experiences of a Humanist mother

by Jane Wynne Willson

The Educational Heretics Series

Published 1997 by Educational Heretics Press
113 Arundel Drive, Bramcote Hills, Nottingham NG9 3FQ

British Cataloguing in Publication Data

Wynne Willson, Jane, 1933-
      Parenting without God: experiences of a humanist
mother
      1. Child rearing 2. Humanism 3. Education
      I Title
      649.1

ISBN   1-900219-11-5

Design and production: Educational Heretics Press

Printed by Esparto Ltd., Slack Lane, Derby

**Educational Heretics Press
exists to question
the dogmas of education in general,
and schooling in particular.**

For Ruth, Peter, Tom and Emma,
who survived our mistakes
and taught us so much

Photograph of Ruth and Emma by Jill Racy

Contents

Introduction

Introduction

"Why do people have to be dead?"
"Miss Higginson says that Grandpa has gone to heaven, so why didn't you tell me that?"
"Is it true that God will punish you if you are naughty?"
"Can I go to Sunday School with Pete?"
"If Jesus loves little children, like Mr. Hawksworth says, why did he let Mandy get leukaemia so that all her hair fell out?"

Most children ask their parents questions like these when the occasion arises and they expect, and deserve, sensible answers. So if you belong to that section of the community who do not hold any religious beliefs at all - about 30% of the population of the UK at the present time - how exactly do you answer your child? Some of these parents would call themselves 'Humanists'; others would simply describe themselves as 'non-religious', agnostic or atheist, and many may not be aware that the Humanist movement exists and is made up of people who share their belief that you can be moral without religion. Throughout the book I have tended to use the term 'Humanist' when referring to all these categories of people.

This short book puts forward a few ideas and suggestions and has been written as the result of a number of requests from parents. Some of them feel isolated in communities where their friends and neighbours all seem to hold different beliefs from their own; all expressed the need for support and advice.

This book is not based on study or research but is the result of practical experience. Every common aspect of child care is already covered in authoritative books written by professionals and experts. I write as a mother of four grown-up children who now have families of their own, and as a retired teacher. I was myself brought up in a family where there was no religion, have been actively involved in the Humanist movement for many years, and know a number of families who feel the same as I do. We all struggled to find ways of explaining things and sought honest answers to children's questions, and could probably have done with a book of this kind ourselves.

I want to highlight areas in a child's upbringing where particular problems may arise or where a Humanist approach tends to be different. But I shall include areas where there is unlikely to be much difference in order to give a more balanced view.

Again and again over recent months there have been articles in the press, programmes on radio and TV and utterances from our political leaders, which bemoan what they like to call the 'moral vacuum' in society and the fecklessness of many parents. They blame this to a large extent on the decline in religious belief and the failure of parents to provide religious and moral guidance. Even supposing one agreed that moral standards are declining, it does not follow that this trend would be reversed by a return to the teaching of so-called 'Christian values', either at home or in school.

In this book I intend to put forward a different view and to suggest that a Humanist approach to child-rearing is a satisfactory and honest one, both for the parents and for the children. I also hope to show that Humanist parenting can provide a firm and sound basis for morality.

Most of the challenges and rewards of parenthood are ones that we share with Christians*. But there are others that are peculiar to us, and ways of looking at things that are fundamentally different. My purpose is not to criticise those of a religious persuasion merely to score points, but only where a comparison seems relevant and helps to clarify an issue. Overall I will try to offer constructive and practical suggestions for handling situations and point out the positive aspects of being a Humanist parent.

Lastly, I would like to stress that there can be no such thing as 'the Humanist view' or 'Humanist policy' over such an intensely personal matter as how you bring up your own children. But I venture to hope that some of the views I put forward strike a chord with other Humanist parents.

[* Throughout the book I tend to refer to 'Christians', when in some instances what I say may equally apply to those who follow other religious traditions. The reason for this is that, historically speaking, we have been 'a Christian country' and it is through its privileged position that the Church of England still affects much of what we do even today.]

Chapter one

Starting a family

Perhaps the most wonderful and exciting thing in the natural world is the ability of living things to reproduce. Among animals, human beings are unique in their capacity to make sophisticated decisions about having babies. The majority of men and women in this country are able to choose whether or not to have a family, how many children they want, when to have them and how to space them. But with this capacity goes grave responsibility.

As they say on the stickers, *'A dog is for life, not just for Christmas.'* The same applies to babies, only very much more so. When two people bring a child into the world, they are taking on a commitment that will last, if not for life, at least during the long years until that tiny, totally dependent baby becomes an adult. In some circumstances the parental responsibility can last much longer than that.

For Humanists the birth of a baby is not a gift of God, nor is a sexual relationship just for the procreation of children. Contraception has made it possible for sex to be enjoyed in its own right. In past generations women struggled to bring up huge and often ailing families. Their only respite from childbirth was when their husbands were 'considerate' - in other words abstained from sex - or else went elsewhere for sexual gratification. These women frequently died young, leaving the eldest daughter, often no more than a child herself, to run the family home. Such situations persist even today in the developing countries and in parts of the world where religions such as Roman Catholicism teach that artificial methods of contraception are wrong. We sometimes forget what we owe to the pioneers of birth control and those who have fought, and are still fighting, against prejudice to make it available to all.

So, for those of us who do not believe in a divine creator, a baby is the tangible result of a sexual act, when both partners are fertile and effective contraception has not been used. When stated as baldly as that it may not sound very romantic, but for a Humanist it presents the bare bones of what childbirth is about. To these bare bones one should add the love and fulfilment that the baby usually - though by no means always - represents, and the joy that surrounds the birth of a wanted baby.

The pressure to have a child

The desire to have a child can be a powerful urge. How else would the human race have evolved? You have only to look at the desperate longing of the infertile, and the medical procedures they are prepared to endure in the hopes of producing a baby. Social pressure from well-meaning friends; from parents, who long to become grandparents; the widely held view, (sometimes unspoken but clearly shown), that a couple is not 'normal' and even selfish, if no baby arrives.

This type of unsolicited interference seems to me wrong and should be resisted. There is evidently a significant minority of people who have no wish to have a family. They may have found fulfilment in a way of life together without children or in work that is not compatible with family life. They may have been put off the idea by observing the limitations that having children has imposed on the lives of their friends and those around them. They may simply not like children, and realise that they would not be good parents. They may have come from unhappy families themselves.

Whatever the reason or combination of reasons, it is certainly not for those of us who want and like children ourselves to exert pressure or to pass comment. This is eminently a matter on which individuals must make up their own minds. And there are more than enough babies being born in the world to make overpopulation one of the most serious threats to human survival.

What kind of family unit?

I should like to make clear that, in talking of 'parents', I am referring to two people, partners with a long-term commitment to each other, who have taken on the responsibility of bringing up children. They may or may not be legally married, and I make no distinction between heterosexual and homosexual parents or between adoptive and birth parents.

In talking of a 'family' I mean the so-called 'nuclear' family, though this does not imply that I consider it necessarily the ideal environment for the developing child. Its evident instability, with more than one in three marriages in this country now ending in separation or divorce, suggests that it is not. An extended family, where other members are closely involved with the child, can provide a very secure background and there are other systems that function well in our own and in different cultures and communities. The particular problems faced by parents of either sex who are bringing up children single-handed are considered in a later chapter.

Preparing for parenthood

It has often been observed that parenthood is probably the most important job that any pair of people is going to undertake during their lives, and the one for which the least training is given. Yet the devisors of our National Curriculum have followed earlier educationalists in omitting Parenting Skills from the list of compulsory subjects in school.

In earlier generations, when families were larger, most children grew up with considerable practical experience of caring for younger children. This is no longer common and many, if not most parents, when handling their baby for the first time, have little idea of how to cope. Grandparents and other members of an extended family are not always at hand to help and advise, as they were for earlier generations.

So new parents, and particularly the new mother, may feel very isolated. The thought of being entirely responsible for another human being can be frightening. After all, it may not be so long ago that you were being looked after by your own parents. You may have only just begun to get used to sharing your life with your partner, and adapting to each other's ways.

And how stable *is* your relationship? Will it stand up to the stresses and strains of having a baby? If you have both been working, will one income or two half incomes be enough to manage on, at least for a time? How will you share the job of looking after the baby? Instead of having to think of the needs of two people, you will have to think of the needs of three people. At first the baby will not be able to express his or her own choices, except to voice the need for food and other creature comforts. So you will be making choices on your baby's behalf.

There is much that can and should be discussed beforehand by couples who want to start a family, for to face likely problems and situations together beforehand is the best way of minimising possible difficulties at a later stage. A mature and rational acceptance of the sacrifices that will need to be made and the changes there will inevitably be will go a long way towards helping parents cope through those early days and months.

I have mentioned some of the changes that the arrival of a baby will undoubtedly bring merely to stress the importance of thinking things through beforehand. I have no wish to play down the intense joy experienced by two people who love each other, when they produce a child together. And I am firmly of the view that the long-lasting pleasures and rewards of having children and the fun of happy family life should, in normal circumstances, far outweigh any temporary problems and anxieties.

Chapter two

The new baby

Pregnancy and childbirth

Book shops and libraries today have a wide selection of books on pregnancy and childbirth. The importance of the health and well-being of the mother both before and during pregnancy is now generally accepted. Over the question of where the baby should be born, much depends on the facilities in different areas, and of course on the circumstances of each case. There *are* choices for some mothers, but for others there is in reality little choice and they must often go along with what their own doctor prefers.

Having had my own children at home, with hospital facilities within easy reach and a GP who was committed to home confinements, I was extremely lucky. If complications had been expected, I would obviously have agreed to a hospital delivery. Indeed, in the event, I did have to go into hospital during labour for our third baby, and all was well. 'Natural' and 'active' birth, where the mother feels more in control of the situation, are an option for some. One of our daughters-in-law had a successful water birth, with the baby floating happily to the surface into the arms of both parents, together in the pool.

'Active birth' is still uncommon in this country, although it has some powerful advocates. Hospital deliveries, with the option of an epidural block to eliminate pain, are still the norm. Caesarian sections, sometimes essential for the safety of the baby, the mother or both, are all too often performed as a more convenient and quicker alternative to natural methods of delivery.

If circumstances are favourable I would imagine that most Humanists would opt for methods which show a greater respect for the human body and its natural processes, and give more responsibility and control to the parents involved. But there will always be exceptions.

Attitudes to childbirth

Not so long ago - certainly within my memory - Church of England vicars regularly held services to 'church' women who had recently given birth. These were not primarily to welcome the new babies and give thanks for their safe delivery, although these feelings were doubtless also expressed. They were for the specific purpose of cleansing the women rendered 'unclean' by the birth. I only mention this as it gives some indication of the breadth of the division between traditional Christian attitudes to women and to natural processes such as birth, and those held by Humanists.

Christianity is not the only religion with a history of regarding women as unclean during menstruation and after childbirth. Muslim women are not allowed to pray or fast while menstruating. In some parts of the world communities have segregated women at these times. Such attitudes are also found among those, for example, who so vehemently opposed the ordination of women. My personal view is that the issues and choices that surround childbirth are much easier for Humanists as we do not share the inheritance of such religious attitudes and dogmas.

Attitudes to breast feeding

One cannot entirely blame religion for the preference of so many mothers to bottle feed. But there can be little doubt that the widespread reluctance to breast feed in modern Western society owes something to the deep-seated feelings of shame over nakedness that have been a feature of Judaeo-Christian thinking. This has been complicated in Western society by the perception of the human breast as being primarily a sexual object. So it is hardly surprising that many women are embarrassed to expose themselves in public. This is exceedingly unfortunate, since there is complete agreement that breast feeding is by far the safest and best for the baby, both physically and psychologically. Certainly the promotion of manufactured baby milk seems to me to be quite immoral, particularly in countries of the developing world where adequate sterilisation of bottles is impossible.

It appears there are very few cases of mothers who cannot breast feed, given the right advice and encouragement from the start. So what we need - from the Humanist movement in particular - is a concerted effort to change public attitudes, so that the sight of a mother feeding her baby in a public place is commonplace and excites no more interest, (or disapproval), than someone drinking a cup of tea. One of my daughters, breast feeding in a train, was asked by the guard if she would like to move to a first class carriage and put the blind down. I suppose the more common the sight of breast feeding becomes, the more it will be felt to be socially acceptable in the Western world, as it is elsewhere.

There is one further point that I would like to make in this matter. When I myself was a baby - bottle fed I am sorry to say - the fashion was to feed babies strictly every four hours. Later this changed to 'feeding on demand', which is nowadays more or less the norm. It has been pointed out to me that demand feeding is the first opportunity that parents can give to their babies to make their own decisions. And this is thoroughly humanist!

Adapting to parenthood

Seemingly constant feeding and dealing with nappies are not the only changes in the life of the new parents! That small person, hopefully so much wanted and dreamed about, has a way of taking over the family from the word go. And this especially applies in the case of the first baby. No more evenings at the cinema, no more visiting friends who are not interested in babies, no more peaceful nights, and often a significant drop in income. Some new parents will find these changes very hard, while others will adapt to their new way of life with ease. It is impossible to predict how individual couples will react - and one never ceases to be surprised.

But for the Humanist parent who has thought rationally before conceiving - one hopes - this planned baby will become part of a family that is not wholly unprepared. In either event, with the baby in a sling or otherwise in tow, it is remarkable what today's parents can achieve. And when there is genuine sharing of responsibility and child care between mother and father, this eases the woman's burden and sacrifice to a large extent.

Welcoming the new baby

Humanist parents, particularly those who were themselves married in a Humanist wedding, may decide to have a Naming Ceremony to welcome the new member of the family. A ceremony held a few weeks or months after the birth provides an opportunity to celebrate the baby's safe arrival and, at the same time, for the parents and others to state their commitment to the child's welfare. It brings relatives and friends together to greet the new member of the family and expresses the importance of the occasion in a formal way. The idea of holding a special ceremony appeals to some parents more than to others, and certainly we never held one for any of ours. But nowadays there is a growing demand for help with planning such ceremonies. To help parents, the British Humanist Association has published a practical guide called *New Arrivals* (See book list).

Choosing supporting adults

Even if there is no formal ceremony, some parents ask two or three special friends to act as 'supporting adults' or 'Friends' to the new child - the secular equivalent of Christian godparents. Their role is twofold: to take a special interest in the child's development and support the parents through the long years to the child's adulthood; and also to be there as a refuge for the child, outside the immediate family circle.

Unlike the Christian godparent, this friend does not make promises on behalf of the infant, nor undertake to see that he or she grows up to be a good Humanist. The commitment is to support both the parents and the child, regularly as well as in times of crisis. For if things do go seriously wrong, for example if one or both parents die or if the marriage comes to grief, someone who is already established as a friend and confidante is an enormous asset, whatever the arrangements made over guardianship.

We were ourselves asked to act as non-godparents to two of our friends' children. Both were conventionally religious but wanted a Humanist input. Naturally we were very pleased to be asked, and made our position absolutely clear *vis-à-vis* the religious side of the task. By agreement we did not attend the Christenings, feeling this was our only option or we would in a way have been conniving at what was going on. Looking back on it I'm afraid we have not been very attentive non-godparents and I feel we *should* have been and it was a lost opportunity.

The disabled child

When a baby is born with a serious congenital abnormality or has been damaged during the birth but survives, there will be many difficult decisions to make. The effect on the parents of having a severely disabled baby which needs their undivided attention can be overwhelming. Where there are other children whose needs can at times be overlooked, the problems are compounded. Support, both of a practical and an emotional kind, from friends as well as from professionals, is absolutely essential.

Neonatal death

Sadly, in a book of this kind, one must also mention the cases where the baby is stillborn, or survives for only a short time. In such tragedies, and also after a miscarriage, it is becoming increasingly common for the parents to choose to hold a funeral ceremony for the baby they have lost. It is now generally accepted that grieving is an essential part of long-term recovery after bereavement, and a funeral ceremony gives parents and the immediate family an opportunity to express their feelings together and to support each other in their grief.

Humanist funeral officiants are always willing to conduct such ceremonies, and advice for those who would prefer to conduct a ceremony themselves, without the presence of a stranger, is available in the British Humanist Association's book, *Funerals Without God.* This contains some positive thoughts that can be expressed even in these tragic situations, and suggests readings and poems.

Chapter three

Building the right foundations

Changing practices in upbringing

As soon as the baby is born, choices about methods of upbringing will have to be made, though it is mostly a matter of common sense and simply following your instinct. Practices change over matters such as how often babies should be fed, whether they should ever be left to cry and whether it is good or bad to let a baby sleep in the parents' bed. Each generation of parents will have their favourite text book which recommends with persuasive authority a particular type of approach. Such books are an enormous standby for parents through all the stages of growing up. They are packed with advice on ways of handling situations, telling parents how to cope with all the common childhood ailments; when to call a doctor, and when there is a simple solution. They teach many of the basic skills needed if one is a parent and exude reassurance and - for the most part - good sense.

Probably the most rational course, when choosing a book, is to select the one whose approach most appeals to you. But it is sensible to be adaptable and prepared to try some alternative approaches, if parts of the advice do not seem to be working for you. A system that suits one baby may not suit another, even within the same family, and it is important not to be too influenced by what happens to be in fashion at the time.

At the risk of generalising rashly, I would guess that Humanist parents would tend towards a child-centred approach, feeding babies when they are hungry, picking them up when they cry, and helping them make their own decisions.

Leanings towards good or evil

The mind of the human baby can no longer be thought of as a clean slate, waiting to be written on, or an empty bucket waiting to be filled. Advances in the understanding of our genetic make-up over the last 100 years have revolutionised our thinking. We now know that the baby is born with a genetic package, which predetermines much of his or her later physical and mental development, and we cannot alter this inheritance. But such basic factors as what we eat, where we live and how we are brought up will also play a significant part in determining the kind of adults we become. And it is in these areas that we can bring influence to bear and must act responsibly.

When it comes to our moral development, interesting questions arise. Does the human infant have the propensity to be good or to be bad? Is his or her moral development genetically predetermined or not? The traditional Christian belief in original sin states that every human being inherits a flawed or 'tainted' nature, with a disposition towards evil behaviour. This appears to be an extension of the Old Testament story of Adam and Eve's expulsion from the Garden of Eden for disobeying God. St. Augustine taught that original sin is transmitted through the sexual act, which is thus brought into disrepute.

So what about a baby born into a Christian household today? It is difficult to believe that any but the most extreme traditionalists can possibly believe that the tiny child they hold in their arms is in some way 'tainted', but there are certainly some that do. More commonly perhaps, at later stages in that child's development when there is behaviour that the parents do not like and probably classify as 'naughty', the deep-rooted belief that the child is 'wicked' can re-emerge. A friend of mine, a Church of England vicar, when discussing the matter with me recently, stated clearly that he believes that the pull towards wrong-doing in a child is stronger than the pull towards moral behaviour, and I have heard others say the same.

It is interesting to speculate how such beliefs came into being, to give rise to the Adam and Eve story in the first place. Babies are completely self-centred, demanding the instant satisfaction of their bodily needs. The shrill and urgent sound of their cries for milk are part of the evolutionary process, no doubt. Those whose cries were weak did not survive. But there is a big difference between the demanding behaviour of very young babies and the belief that they are in some way 'tainted'.

I have a rather more optimistic view about the human baby without, I hope, being starry-eyed. On BBC Radio a few years ago I heard an expert on child development describing *'the natural empathy with people that children are born with.'* [Professor Elizabeth Newsom formerly Head of the Child Development Research Unit at Nottingham University. Broadcast on Radio 4, November 1993]. I liked that description. Anyone who has any dealings with babies is familiar with their ready response to their parents' smile and, at a later stage, their wish to please.

Children, and adults too, *feel* good when they give pleasure to others, as well as when they experience a kindness. Surely the potential for the development of good moral sense is present in all human beings when they are born and, if that is cherished and nurtured along with all other aspects of the personality, a morally aware adult will emerge? In evolutionary terms too, the selective advantage of this human development is essential.

The 'good' child

So what exactly is meant by a 'good' child? The first time I thought seriously about this was many years ago when I was visiting the ward of a children's hospital. There were two little boys there who had just had the same operation. One was a baby of a few days or weeks; the other a child of about six. The older boy was crying bitterly and was clearly in severe pain; the baby was sleeping peacefully. "Why can't you be a good boy like Jamie? Look! He's not making such a fuss", said a nurse. It was so clearly the case that the baby was not in pain at that moment and was also too young to be really frightened at what was happening. There was no *virtue* in the baby's behaviour, nor *naughtiness* in the small boy's distress.

When parents describe their baby as 'good', they are saying that he sleeps and feeds well and does not cry much, if at all. They are in fact saying that their baby is contented and not causing them any trouble. 'Good' is not an appropriate word, though it is the first one that springs to mind and is commonly used in this context. I do not myself believe there can be 'good' or 'bad' babies. Equally, when older children do wrong, the reaction is often to say "You horrible girl!" or, "You stupid boy!" when it is what they *do*, or *how they behave* that is antisocial or 'bad', and not the children themselves who are wicked. This may be a small thing but, as we know from what happens in broken homes where children have a tendency to blame themselves, their self image can be easily damaged.

The 'terrible twos'

It is when the toddler first begins to develop the ability to move about, and later to talk, that problems of management can arise and the seeds of future discord can be sown. The problem lies more with the parents than the child. If the parent interprets the toddler's behaviour as 'wilfulness' or 'naughtiness' and reacts strongly, this can exacerbate the whole situation.

What the so-called 'naughty' children of this age are doing is to explore everything within reach, which is of course an essential stage in their learning. They will later go on to test their parents and find out how they react. Often this is a thinly disguised and potentially very effective move to attract attention to themselves. When there is a new baby in the family, such tactics are almost universal and serve to remind the parents that they must find time to give extra love and attention to the older child, who is feeling displaced.

Sibling rivalry

Jealousy when there is a new baby is to be expected, particularly when it is the first child who has been 'ousted'. There are some points to remember here. This jealousy is perfectly natural from a child who has been up till then at the centre of the stage. It does not show a nasty streak in the toddler's character, and should be ignored, in so far as that is compatible with the new baby's safety.

Some parents seem to me extremely thoughtless and lacking in sensitivity in this situation, and I have witnessed some blatant examples of this, especially in trains! The parent - and in my experience it is usually the mother - is positively drooling over the young baby. The toddler, who may for the last two or three years have enjoyed her full-time attention and devotion, is virtually ignored and visibly distressed. As is inevitable, the toddler starts to 'mess about' and is spoken to crossly, sometimes very angrily. This is particularly the case when the 'messing about' has involved some aggression towards the baby. The mother then returns to her drooling. Small wonder that the seeds of sibling rivalry and often dislike are well and truly sown.

I am not suggesting that parents - and indeed grandparents and others involved with the family - should ignore the new baby, merely that they should make a special fuss of the older child or children as well, to compensate in so far as they can for the arrival on the scene of the little intruder. In small ways too, a little sensitivity about how the toddler is feeling, can be helpful. A suggestion I have heard is that parents should make a point of saying "*our* baby", including the child in the word 'our'. There is much that can be done to involve the older child in helping to care for the baby - changing, dressing, bathing, playing - so that it all becomes a joint enterprise.

The art of diversion

So how should the parent react when the toddler is acting in an antisocial way? The straightforward answer is that, however knowing children may be, it is almost invariably possible to distract them. With babies the distraction can be very basic: picking them up, producing a different toy, singing, clapping - almost anything will be effective and the original cause of the trouble will usually be forgotten at once. For the older child the distracting technique must be marginally more subtle, and forward planning to avoid situations is helpful. So, on journeys, take an assortment of occupations and favourite toys and books, and be prepared to give your own time to playing with and talking with the child. So many parents seem to have no idea of the tedium young children will feel when made to endure what seem to them interminable waits. Boredom, and antisocial behaviour as the direct result of boredom, is plainly the fault of the parent who has not had the imagination to realise what the child is experiencing. It is another all too common example of parent-induced 'naughtiness'.

Rules - and the reasons for rules

As the child develops, Humanist parents will probably opt for very few family 'rules' and only ones that are soundly based and can be explained to the child even at a basic level. They would not be likely to go in for the, "Do this, or else", or the, "because I say so!" kind of approach. It is usually possible to devise strategies for dealing with situations.

Such rules as there are will mostly be for the protection of the child; sometimes they will be for the protection of the parent! For example, in the latter category, a child may be expected to understand at the appropriate age, that their parents are not best pleased at being woken up in the night, unless they are really needed. If they are short of sleep they may be grumpy in the morning.

The protection of the small child from the hazards of traffic, fire and water, is essential. But it must be borne in mind that overprotection in activities such as climbing and exploring can produce a nervous and clumsy child who lacks self-confidence, and has poor awareness and judgement of what constitutes a real danger. Stair gates are an example. We had four gates, I remember, in a tall Bristol house. Our grandchildren do not have them at all, and none of them have had serious falls. As one of my daughters pointed out to me, puppies and kittens never fall down stairs, so why should babies?

Chapter four

Setting the right example

I have mentioned diversionary tactics for the very young, when antisocial or unpleasant behaviour is used as an attention seeking device. I have also suggested that too many rules, other than the minimum needed for safety, are not a good idea, and that a reason should be given if possible, whenever you find yourself saying: "No! don't do that!" If a parent is going to refuse or prohibit something, then it seems to me important that they do not waver. If they *are* going to relent, this must be done at once. Otherwise it can easily lead to the wheedling one so often hears at the supermarket checkout, where the immoral placing of chocolate bars causes many an exhausted parent to kow-tow to their plaintive offspring. There is nothing worse than children who perpetually whine, in the knowledge that if they go on long enough, they will eventually get what they want. Bribery as a method of getting children to do something they do not want to do is used by all parents from time to time, even if it is only over such a small thing as giving a sweet after foul-tasting medicine - and some of these life-saving antibiotics certainly taste vile! To use bribery as a technique too often would seem to me to be unwise, but negotiation with give and take on both sides can be used to good effect - at any age!

Learning by imitation

So what *is* the most effective way of getting a child to recognise what constitutes acceptable behaviour - in the commonly used phrase, to 'learn the difference between right and wrong'? The answer seems to me obvious: if you speak to children gently, show them love and respect in the way you handle them, and let them observe you interacting with others in a considerate and friendly way, then this is the kind of behaviour they will naturally adopt.

Consider the amount learned and absorbed by a child during the first few years of life, and how this is achieved. The powers of memory of an average child are phenomenal - especially when compared with those of an average middle-aged adult! Children need hear a word used only once or twice and, so long as they understand its meaning, they will remember and use it. Similarly their imitative powers are astonishing, and they will ape and reproduce much of what goes on around them. If shown affection, they will return affection; if smacked, they will smack back, (either the person who smacked them, or someone else); if other children draw on the wall, they will do the same.

There was a series on television a while ago called *Nanny Knows Best* in which some very brave parents who were having problems with young children asked the advice of an ex-nanny. In one episode we were shown an extremely unruly toddler misbehaving outrageously, while the wretched mother attempted to wheel him round the supermarket in a trolley. He was shrieking and kicking and generally creating a scene. The mother was shouting at him, threatening him and was clearly very embarrassed by his behaviour. Subsequently, when Nanny's advice was sought, her first comment to the mother was: "Well of course, he's just like you." And later, we were shown the same little boy, quiet and happy, being taken round the same supermarket by Nanny, who was involving him in what she was choosing from the shelves, getting him to help her, and talking all the while in a calm, normal voice.

Learning from parents

Harold Blackham, the first Director of the British Humanist Association, wrote some 30 years ago in his classic book *'Humanism'*:

> ' ... *the experience parents give a child does more harm or good than anything that is said or not said. That experience comes from the way the child is treated and the way the parents behave and live. A child who enjoys affection, understanding, interest and never-failing encouragement, without being left to be ruled by his own drives or allowed to rule the house, will have favourable soil in which to root and*

thrive ... Parents' own behaviour should include complete honesty about their own views and the manifest attempt to live in the light of them.'

Achieving the ideal

The Humanist parent, as has already been said, is not encumbered with the belief that there is a tendency towards evil in the young child; rather the reverse. We accept that characteristics and tendencies are often inherited and that in some cases this may present problems. We also accept that it is our responsibility to provide the best possible environment for the growing child. If we are now of the view that moral behaviour is largely taught by example, then we have before us a straightforward practical programme for helping the young child grow into an adult who is morally aware.

What is there to prevent us following such a programme? Situations and circumstances may work against us. Over-crowding, poverty, isolation, ill health, and stress are only some of the social difficulties that may make the ideals I have described impossible to achieve. Also we are all human and, as such, incapable of keeping up high standards of behaviour at all times, however much we know them to be right. Nor need we. Children, as is often said, are pretty resilient and will not be affected by the odd lapse or occasion when we have lost our patience. What is more it is important that they should realise that even their parents behave badly at times, or they will be living in *Cloud Cuckoo Land* and themselves striving towards a goal that is impossible to reach.

Perhaps parents should be more prepared to apologise to their children when they treat them unfairly. To give a simple example: suppose you are completely exhausted after spending an hour cleaning the kitchen floor, and Percy, your two-year-old, wanders in from the garden in muddy boots. You shout at him, pick him up firmly and dump him back in the garden.

Percy bursts into tears. When you have calmed down and cleared up the mess, you realise that you overreacted absurdly to what he did, simply because you were tired. If someone else had cleaned the floor or if you had not been exhausted, your reaction would have been different. You owe Percy an apology and an explanation. Children need to know that their parents are fallible.

Not in front of the children

The total honesty advocated by Harold Blackham is a useful rule of thumb and is probably the norm in most Humanist families. There will be subjects, however, that are best discussed without the children there, such as matters that will cause them unnecessary concern or fear. In families where the parents indulge in bitter quarrels in front of the children, or within their earshot, the effect can be traumatic and the damage long-lasting. Where one parent disagrees with something the other has said or done that affects the children, I would think this is best not discussed in front of them. It is important not to give conflicting instructions or undermine each other's authority.

Chapter five

Distinguishing fact from fiction

Everyone likes a good story. Throughout history there have been
myths and stories passed down from generation to generation by
word of mouth, later in story books and nowadays on television
and radio as well. The world of fantasy plays an essential part in
children's lives, developing their powers of imagination and
opening their eyes to a wider world and richer experiences. Tales
of monsters and giants, of princesses and witches, of pirates and
spaceships, may be where children first feel some of the strongest
human emotions and begin to understand why people behave as
they do.

The world of make-believe

At the same time as accepting and even entering into the fantasy
world of their children with games and story telling, parents can
help them distinguish fact from fiction. With care, this can
usually be done without treating the characters and experiences of
the imagination as in some way inferior to those in real life, thus
belittling them.

The myth of Father Christmas

So what is the difference between 'playing along with' a child's
fantasy and presenting a mythical character such as Father
Christmas as fact? As children, my sisters and I knew, even from
a very young age, that parents were the people who crept into
bedrooms and put full stockings at the end of the beds. We also
knew that some of our friends believed in Father Christmas, or
professed to do so. As parents, my husband and I were certainly
reproached by a few people for depriving our children of some of
the 'magic' of Christmas. But my children have assured me that
this was certainly not so and that they still find Christmas, fun!

But there are a few questions that spring to mind. For example, how pleasant is it to lie in bed, waiting for a stranger to climb down the chimney, even if he is laden with gifts? What if you have no chimney in your room, like most of today's children? Will it be the same old man whom you queued up to see in town on Saturday, whose face you could see behind his Santa mask and whose beery breath you could smell? Children are always warned never to take sweets from strangers! And again, what if you did something pretty awful on Christmas Eve, such as punching your brother so that his nose bled? Everyone knows, and people in shops are always telling you, that Father Christmas visits only *good* children. Daddy says that it is true about Father Christmas, so it must be, because Daddy doesn't tell lies.

What a lot of confusion! And all because the boundary between fact and fiction has become blurred. Would it not be more honest if the child is told that it is a story - a nice story shared by children in many parts of the world - but still a *story*? Is not that a magical thought, that children in far off lands also hang up their stockings, or in some cases put out their shoes, though in some countries they do it on a different day? Your family give you presents at Christmas because it is a custom, and as soon as you are old enough you make or buy small gifts for them. There is no tie-up with being good. Your parents love you for who you are, not for what you do.

The comfort of fantasy

Many of the well known fairy tales, such as *Little Red Riding Hood* and *Cinderella,* cross international boundaries, and can be found in different countries. Children who are uprooted and are consequently unsettled or unhappy, can find continuity and comfort in the world of fantasy, which remains unchanged. My adopted sister, who came to this country from central Europe as a refugee at the age of five, has told me that the familiar fairy tales she found here were a great comfort. Alone in a foreign country, they were one of the few links with her past.

Children quite often have an imaginary 'friend' to play with, and the 'friend' may be part of the family circle for years, with his place laid at the table and his special chair by the fire. Some children regularly take on the role of an imaginary character themselves, and get very angry if others do not address them in their character part.

The religious 'myths'

Bible stories and tales from the other world religions slot happily into this familiar, imaginary world of childhood. So when your child comes home from primary school and asks you whether Jesus really *did* walk on the water, you can answer with complete honesty that you think it was rather like some of the magic things that happen in the fairy story books. For the older child you can even explain how, when story telling was an art, what appeared to be simple stories often concealed more important ideas and deeper moral truths. Some of these Bible stories are of that type, like the story of the Good Samaritan.

At these early stages, any conflict of belief between home and school should not present too many problems. It may already have arisen at home or among friends. A child will usually accept the answer: "Well, Miss Higginson seems to believe that Jesus really did these things, and you know that Grandma does as well, but Dad and I think it was probably only a very nice story." Similar conflicts may arise between what is taught in different lessons at school. I heard of a child who learned about the law of gravity in the physics lesson one morning and the resurrection of Jesus in RE the same afternoon! He came home asking which he should believe. In cases like this, when there is a problem reconciling opposing or differing views, one must reassure the child that there is no need for him to make up his mind until he is much older - there is plenty of time for him to think about the reasons for believing one thing or another. One can stress how important it is to keep an open mind, and to be prepared to change one's view, as grown ups often do, when there is new evidence and new thinking.

Learning to tell the truth

"This story telling is all very well", I can hear you saying, "but how can children learn the importance of telling the truth? How can they distinguish between telling stories for enjoyment and telling lies out of mischief?"

The answer must be that, as soon as the child is old enough to understand, it is up to the parents, and later the teacher, to make the difference absolutely clear. Most children will soon learn to recognise when something is in the realm of fiction. However, so that the boundary between the two does not become blurred, the responsible parent does not delude the child into believing that there really *are* fairies at the bottom of the garden. And, as I have already mentioned, it does seem to me, personally, that carrying on the myth of Father Christmas too seriously is bordering on the irresponsible.

Truthfulness is one of the main characteristics of a Humanist parent. I would suggest that the only justifiable exceptions are in situations where to tell the whole truth would cause unnecessary hurt or fear. These exceptions would normally consist of watering down or avoiding the truth. For example, when one of my children at the age of about eight bought me an unspeakably hideous purple dress at a jumble sale which she clearly thought was lovely, I obviously pretended that I thought so too. If a woman became HIV positive after being reckless on a Mediterranean holiday, she would not want to tell her three year old child the full story. This kind of 'economy with the truth' and to what extent it is justifiable, is eminently a matter for discussion when the child is much older.

Chapter six

The rights of the child

Children are individuals and deserve as much respect as adults. This should not need saying, but alas, it does. Throughout history, up to and including the present day, in societies all over the world, countless children have been badly treated by adults. How has this been justified? Well, we adults are bigger and stronger and, in many respects, we know better. In any case it is for the child's good to find out that life is hard and to learn self discipline. Or so they say ...

This maltreatment has amounted at best to bullying and suppression and at worst to exploitation and cruelty. Child labour on a massive scale is still a world problem and, in some of the poorest countries, families survive only through the meagre earnings of their children, many of whom work long hours in appalling conditions, some as young as six years old.

This can no longer be done with impunity. Children's rights are now enshrined in international law and those who transgress lay themselves open to criminal prosecution. On the 20th November 1989, the Convention on the Rights of the Child was adopted by the United Nations General Assembly. It entered into force the following year, after being ratified by more nations than any human rights declaration before. The Convention contains 54 articles in all. I shall summarise the 13 which seem to me the most relevant to the subject of my book.

Article 3. The best interests of the child

All actions concerning the child should take full account of his or her best interests. The State is to provide adequate care when the parents or others responsible fail to do so.

Article 5. Parental guidance

The State has a duty to respect the rights and responsibilities of parents and the wider family to provide guidance appropriate to the child's evolving capacities.

Article 12. The child's opinion

The child has the right to express an opinion, and to have that opinion taken into account, in any matter or procedure affecting him or her.

Article 13. Freedom of expression

The child has the right to obtain and make known information, and to express his or her views, unless this would violate the rights of others.

Article 14. Freedom of thought, conscience and religion

The child has the right to freedom of thought, conscience and religion, subject to appropriate parental guidance and national law.

Article 15. Freedom of association

Children have the right to meet with others and to join or set up associations, unless the fact of doing so violates the rights of others.

Article 16. Protection of privacy

The child has the right to protection from interference with privacy, family, home and correspondence, and from libel and slander.

Article 17. Access to appropriate information

The media is responsible for disseminating to children only such information as is consistent with moral well-being and knowledge and understanding among people; it must respect the cultural background of all children and protect them from harmful materials.

Article 18. Parental responsibilities

The State should ensure recognition of the principle that both parents have common responsibilities for the upbringing and development of their child. The best interests of the child will be their basic concern. The State must ensure that children of working parents have the right to benefit from child care services and facilities for which they are eligible.

Article 19. Protection from abuse and neglect

The State is obliged to protect children from all forms of maltreatment perpetrated by the parents or others responsible for their care, and to undertake preventative and treatment programmes in this area.

Article 27. Standard of living

Children have the right to enjoy an adequate standard of living and parents have the primary responsibility for this. The State has a duty to ensure that this responsibility can be, and is being, fulfilled.

Article 28. Education

The child has the right to an education that is free and compulsory, at least at the primary stage. School discipline should reflect the child's human dignity.

Article 29. Aims of education

The education of the child should be directed at developing the child's personality and talents, preparing for adult life; it should foster respect for the child's parents, his or her own cultural and national values and those of others; it should prepare the child for responsible life in a free society; it should develop in the child a respect for the natural environment.

The relevance for Humanist parents

All the articles referred to above will, I feel sure, find sympathy with Humanist parents. Perhaps of particular interest are Articles 12, 13 and 14. In our current educational climate and under the present law, children from Humanist and non-religious homes frequently have their need for moral guidance neglected in schools. Christian-dominated assemblies and religious education tend to be the order of the day, with a fragment of time allowed to learn about festivals from other world religions. Certainly, there are open-minded and fair teachers who do take the opinions of children from Humanist homes into account, but there are others who do not and we have a long way to go until all teaching in this area is, *'objective, fair and balanced.'* This is often the fault of the curriculum rather than of those who have to teach to it.

Children expressing a Humanist view, which they may have heard at home or worked out for themselves, are seldom taken seriously and are sometimes rebuked and patronised. When this happens, it is certainly in contravention of Articles 12 and 13 of the Convention, and parents are well within their rights to point this out if they are aware that it is going on and are concerned about the effect on their child.

Article 14, giving children the right to, 'freedom of thought, conscience and religion', is also well worth bearing in mind if one feels one's child is being subjected to religious indoctrination to a damaging extent. When children from Humanist families are refused admission to the Guide or Scout movement, it might be helpful to quote this Article and also Article 15. This issue is further discussed in Chapter 11.

Chapter seven

Coping with death

How to explain death to children is one of the hardest tasks faced by all parents. In the case of Humanist parents, people tend to think that it is a disadvantage that we do not have ready words of comfort, such as, "Your Grandma has gone to heaven to be with Jesus". This answer is naturally assumed to comfort the child, because heaven is a nice place where horrid things do not happen and nice things do - for example Grandma will meet Grandpa again. In fact the reverse is possibly the case and in some ways Humanists have the easier option. We do not have to find reasons to explain how an all-loving and all-powerful God could allow such a thing to happen, "when Grandma was looking forward to coming to stay with us". We do not have to explain how it will be possible to meet up with someone whom we know was reduced to ashes at the crematorium, or was buried in the ground. Humanists and Christians alike will have to handle the grief, regardless of their different beliefs, and its severity will depend on the closeness of the relationship that was severed by the death. It might be helpful to look in detail at the three major problem areas. First, your children will want to know what actually happens when someone dies; they will want some explanation of why this is so; and lastly, and perhaps most importantly, all children need help in coping with their grief.

The fact of death

However you look at it, death is a stark fact. To come to terms with the knowledge that life is finite and that, after you die, there is nothingness, is hard enough for adults. One might expect it to be even harder for children, who have little concept of a natural order in which birth and death are an ever recurring process. But often children surprise us by what they can take in their stride, and we are left stunned by their apparent resilience and acceptance of whatever comes along.

How can one best explain the harsh reality? Different people will use different approaches, depending on the individuals and the relationships concerned, the ages of the children, and other factors. I will make a few suggestions.

Most children nowadays will have experienced death in stories, films and on television from an early age. But that does not directly involve them and their first actual contact with death may well be the loss of a pet. Even very young children are often deeply attached to a pet animal, whether their own or not. The pet may be anything from a dog to a stick insect, but it can be the object of that child's devotion. If it dies, there will be real grief. In the case of pets, it is important that children are told their expected life span, and know that, when they grow old and probably ill, they will die. This understanding is then naturally and easily transferred to the prospect of people dying, in all probability their grandparents or elderly relations. If a close relative or friend is nearing death, either from a fatal illness or failing health, it must surely be better for children in the family to be aware of the impending death than to be protected from what is happening. The death will not then come as an unexpected shock. It is so easy to assume that children should be sheltered from the grievous things of life.

But evidence suggests that to exclude them totally from anxious family situations and shared grieving can be far more damaging in the long run. I know a young woman who, at the age of seven, was with her younger brother when he was killed in an accident. She was not allowed to attend the funeral and was told by a nun at school that her brother was in heaven and she could talk to him any time. Often during the next few years, she used to hide in a cupboard and hold long conversations with her brother. Otherwise, she seldom spoke. It was not until she was 14 that someone told her the truth - that her brother was dead and she would never see him again. The psychological damage done to this girl, who was not allowed or helped to grieve, emerged many years later.

To go back to the actual explanation, it is vital to get across to children that, once a person is dead, there is no pain. The commonest way people explain death is to liken it to being asleep, but without the dreams or any prospect of waking up. There is a built-in difficulty here, that some children become fearful of going to sleep themselves or of seeing others asleep, and need much reassurance over this. The absence of pain can be a great comforter if the person who has died was seen suffering. Adults are often surprised, or even shocked, by the questions children may ask about what happens to the dead body, and their evident fascination about it. One should not be surprised, for children learn by asking questions and getting truthful answers. For earlier generations death was not the taboo subject it is today in this country, and also a more everyday occurrence. Babies and young children died tragically often, mothers died in childbirth, and people died in their beds and not in hospital. The dead body remained in the house for several days in the open coffin, for people to take their last farewells. The children, along with everyone else, could see the dead person lying peacefully there, and there was little mystery about it. Nowadays, this is seldom the case, and the only way children can find out what is going on is by asking. If there is to be a burial, they will want to know what happens to the body under the ground; if it is to be cremated, they will want to know the details and will need reassurance that no pain is involved. One of our own grandsons, who was nearly three at the time, found it difficult to dissociate burning from pain. He needed a lot of reassurance about this when his great grandmother, to whom he was very attached, was cremated.

"Why do people have to die?"

Even with children as young as three or four it should be possible to explain, in very simple and concrete terms, something of the natural cycle and even a basic version of the theory of evolution. These days the task is made easier by their familiarity with the concept of recycling, and their greater awareness of the natural environment. As soon as they start school, and often before, children learn about the seasons, the dying of the old year in Autumn, the rebirth in Spring, and all that goes with it. They know about flowers and trees, lambs and other young life, so it is not so hard for them to see how human beings fit into the natural pattern. Babies are being born all the time, probably within their own family circle, and old people die. What is so different? A Humanist parent I know, reported that her seven year old son has asked to be buried in the garden, and to have a buddleia tree planted over his grave, "then butterflies will come and fly around, and I will be one of them". Perhaps he had been learning about Buddhism at school!

It is much harder to explain sudden death such as an accident or suicide, and the deaths of children and young people are particularly difficult. One can only be honest, and comfort the child as best one can. If there is an element of relief in the death, for example that the person had been in great pain and that this would have got worse, then this aspect can be stressed. Obviously if there is not a positive side to stress it would be wrong to invent one. In the case of an accident or suicide, it is important that there should never be any element of blame attached to the child, as we know that children have a tendency to think things are their fault. Soon enough they will understand and accept that good things happen and bad things happen, and that is the way life is. One cannot always attach meaning to events.

It is rather a tall order to try to explain to a young child why it is necessary for people like other living things to die, in order for the human race to survive and adapt. It should not be impossible, however, if their questions probe deeply and they are interested in such fundamental issues.

You can give an account of how we have slowly adapted over millions of years to become the amazingly highly developed species that we are today. If you look together at pictures of early ape men, you can point out some striking differences. They have flatter brows, because their brains were much smaller; they have a lot of body hair, because they needed warmth for their way of life; they were only just beginning to make and use tools - so different from computer technology today. And so forth. All these developments could happen only because of the continuing sequence of birth and death, which makes it possible for all living things to adapt over a long period to a changing environment. So, you see, if people did not die, the human race would have come to an end long ago, (or words to that effect).

Helping children cope with grief

Bereavement counselling is now well established in this country, and there are specialist counsellors to help children who have suffered particularly tragic bereavement. There is a much greater awareness and understanding of the short and long-term effects of death on children.

Some important points should be remembered here. The first one is that, when a parent dies, there is a natural tendency for much sympathy and support to be focused on the surviving partner or spouse. It is vital that the urgent needs of the children should not be overlooked. Secondly, some people have felt it kinder to exclude children from a family death, perhaps by sending them away to relations until after the funeral is over and things are back to 'normal'. This is now widely recognised to be unwise, and it is thought better for the child to share in the grieving, attend the funeral, and feel part of the family through sad as well as happier times. Depending on the children's age, they can be given practical, helpful jobs to do, which will make them feel wanted and useful. For example, cakes or sandwiches will need making if people are coming back to the house after the funeral; a poem may have to be copied out; or Grandma may need company.

If the funeral is a Humanist, non-religious ceremony, this takes the form of a celebration of the dead person's life. When the ceremony is being planned, there is usually much talk of the person who has died, and a pooling of anecdotes to be used in the tribute. Children often suggest items - favourite sayings, funny episodes or stories, a special bit of music or a poem - and sometimes they want to contribute to the ceremony themselves.

The process of thinking back to happy times is a help in coming to terms with a death. A ceremony is a practical example of the importance of the memories that we leave in other people's minds. These are what remain; this is the only immortality in which Humanists believe. And this, incidentally, is an excellent reason for striving to act in a way that will ensure that the memories we leave behind of ourselves will be largely good and happy ones!

Remembering the person who has died

When a child has lost their mother or father, I have heard the suggestion that the surviving parent, or perhaps a grandparent or other relation or friend, can make them a little book with photos and stories about the parent that has died. The child can derive comfort from this personal treasure, their own special link with the mother or father they have lost. Sometimes a parent who knows they will die soon can do this themselves, which will make it even more precious.

This leads naturally to another important matter: talking freely about the relation or friend long after the funeral is over. Humanist officiants often point out in their address that so-and-so will always be part of the family, the circle, or whatever is relevant. Now this cannot be so in real terms, we know, and it cannot even figuratively be so if the person in question is never referred to. In the case of children who have lost one or both parents in early childhood this is especially important. If they do not remember the parent themselves they rely totally on what they can glean from people who do. And I know of no-one who does not want to get a feel for what the missing parent was like and to find out things about their own mother or father's life.

I have personal experience of this. My own father died when I was a few months old and, until she died at the age of 90, my mother found it virtually impossible to talk about him to us. This was in spite of, or perhaps because of, the fact that she had lost her own mother at the age of three and that her father, who also never remarried, had behaved in exactly the same way with his three children. This left a void in the lives of the children of both generations, which I feel sure would have been less traumatic if talking about the missing parent had not been more or less taboo. I know it had a long term effect on me. I still find it hard - 60 years on - to think or speak of my father without distress.

Chapter eight

Authority and discipline

What kind of discipline?

People talk a lot about the need for discipline when bringing up children. They lay the blame for the increase in various types of crime among young people on the lack of discipline in the home. Such people are usually referring to an authoritarian kind of discipline involving punishment - including physical punishment - when a child has done wrong or has acted in a way that they consider 'disobedient'. Fear of punishment by a parent or teacher is still thought by many to be the best way of teaching a child to behave well and grow up to be an honest and upright citizen. This follows the approach enshrined in many of the world religions which teach their followers that God will punish them if they do not obey his rules.

In my view this method of trying to instil morality into children through fear can have serious drawbacks. As well as being unpleasant and thoroughly unhumanistic, it can achieve quite the opposite result to what was intended. In the first place some children soon develop a protective layer, so the shouts and threats simply have no effect. Also, when the authority figure - the parent or teacher - is not there, the child will often run wild. As an ex-teacher myself I know that some of the pupils most difficult to handle at school are those who come from homes where severe punishment is doled out. Such children see more liberal, humane approaches as weakness, simply because they are not used to being treated with consideration and respect, as rational beings who are responsible for how they act.

Other sanctions and alternative approaches

Clearly, all children will need to be 'told off' at times and, from the age of perhaps three or even before, I have learned that it is best to sit down straight away with the child and talk seriously, firmly and, (one hopes), calmly, about what has just happened. If the child is actually kicking and screaming, it may be a good idea to hold them until they have calmed down. If, as is usually the case, the parent is not alone with the child, it is better if possible to go somewhere away from other people for this serious conversation. You may want to ask *why* they did what they did, and to explain why it was unacceptable.

If another person was involved, the child will usually agree to go and apologise. It may be a very perfunctory apology, as in the case of my two 3-year-old grandsons Charlie and Zaki when they had a fight the other day. Charlie had got hurt and after some persuasion Zaki reluctantly agreed to say he was sorry, adding "..but I want to hit Charlie first .."

If something has been broken, the child can help mend it, if it is mendable. Sometimes, it may be necessary to withdrawal a treat or privilege, but I do feel that even this element of punishment should never be allowed to last long. "Wait till your Dad comes home", seems to me appalling from every point of view. Perhaps the *worst* thing the parent can do is to withdraw their affection from the miscreant. One must remember to inveigh against what the child has *done* - "That really was a silly thing to do", or, "That was not a very kind thing to say!" I fully realise that this is a counsel of perfection and I have certainly called children "stupid" and "dreadful" many times, but since the distinction was pointed out to me by one of my daughters, I have tried very hard not to repeat the mistake.

As with all aspects of parenting, much will depend on the character of the individual child, and what works for one child may not work for another. Professional help with behavioural problems may sometimes need to be sought.

The need for guidelines and boundaries

I am sure it is right that children need clear guidelines and boundaries. To give children and young adolescents complete freedom to act as they like is not doing them any kindness at all. As has been mentioned in an earlier chapter, Humanist families tend to justify what rules they have with good reasons wherever possible, and to avoid the, "because I say so", approach.

For example, it is *reasonable* for children not to wander off without their parents knowing where they are going. It is *reasonable* for parents to insist that children eat sweets only at certain times. It is *reasonable* for children to do their homework before they go out to play and go to bed at an agreed time. In all these situations sensible reasons can be given.

In the case of older children, rules are less likely to be ignored or rebelled against if they are established after sensible discussion between all parties, perhaps with compromises on both sides and a certain amount of negotiation. I would think that parents are wise if they allow leeway and bend rules in exceptional circumstances.

A united front

In the area of discipline I do believe it is important for parents to present a united front. Very early on, children try to play one parent off against the other, and it is clearly a good thing if they are unsuccessful in this ploy. On occasions one parent may think that the other has made the wrong decision, but even so it is generally a mistake to point this out in front of the child, as this can seriously undermine their partner's authority. Soon enough every child will become aware that different adults react differently, and that certain things will annoy one parent more than the other. Children also learn that behaviour which is acceptable at home is not necessarily appropriate in other people's homes. They will need guidance over this - it is largely a matter of sensitivity.

Chapter nine

'Mixed' marriages

Most of this book is written about families where both parents are Humanist. In this chapter I am specifically dealing with 'mixed' marriages, by which I mean a marriage or partnership where one of the parties holds religious beliefs and the other does not. I cannot claim to speak with any personal experience in this matter. Among our friends and family, however, we know a number of marriages where there are conflicts of belief, and I have talked with some of these people to hear how they coped to minimise the tensions and avoid the problems that we all know can arise.

Planning ahead

What emerged as the most important thing of all, was the need to think ahead and foresee areas of difficulty, so that compromised solutions can be agreed in advance. The wedding itself is often the first hurdle, and if that can be sorted out without too much hard feeling or any rifts within the wider family, this must be a good omen. Even when there are no fundamental differences of belief, planning a wedding with all its ramifications can be stressful, and this further dimension may make things extremely difficult.

A situation in which my husband and I have recently become involved concerns an engagement between Anne, a young woman brought up in a Catholic family, and Paul, who has no religious faith. In every other respect the couple are absolutely right for each other and seem destined for a happy marriage, and they are sensibly trying to break down this barrier between them many months before the proposed wedding. Paul sought our advice as Humanists about various difficulties that were worrying him.

The wedding was the first problem. There was no question of a full Roman Catholic service as he himself had never been christened, (let alone baptised into the Catholic church), and he was unwilling to go through with all that - nor, to be fair, was Anne expecting him to. She was prepared to make do with a simplified service, more in the nature of a blessing, which was obviously a considerable sacrifice on her part. Paul seemed prepared to go along with this so long as he was not put in the position of having to say something that he did not believe, and so long as the service included some kind of token secular or Humanist section.

A major problem was that Anne, although not an active Catholic herself, feels it an essential part of her life, and she considers that, in its place, Paul has a 'void'; namely, that an absence of religion is mere nothingness. When she expresses this view it upsets him considerably. It was clear that neither of them had any intention of trying to convert the other, which seemed sensible to us. Our *advice* was more in the nature of support and encouragement, as Paul had already thought deeply about how he felt and how best they could sort things out between them.

His aim was to try to persuade Anne that they must *both* try to understand and respect each other's beliefs, even though they could not share them. At the same time he would insist that, within their marriage, Humanism should have equal status with Catholicism. We encouraged him to take a strong stand over this. They are so determined to break down the barrier while at the same time keeping their own integrity, that we feel hopeful that they will manage to work something out together.

The status of Humanism

I feel that establishing the status of Humanism is the crux of the matter. Humanists may have considerable difficulty getting their religious partners to realise that Humanism fulfils *for them* the role that religion does for religious people. They need to accept that it is not a negative quantity, but a well established stance for living and a sound basis for morality.

A deeply committed Humanist whom I know, married to a practising Anglican, has explained to me that he and his wife have not had too much difficulty as she takes a liberal, non-dogmatic approach to his Humanist beliefs, and they both from the start agreed to differ. He describes them as sharing the same set of values, although these come from different sources, and as sharing the view that their children should have a 'balanced opportunity to make up their own minds' and should be given the necessary information to enable them to do this. So she provides the religious input that is so important to her and he provides the antidote - using remarks such as, "Well, that is what some people think, but others believe ..." Apparently this is all done by mutual agreement and without rancour, and seems to me the ideal way of coping with the situation.

Christenings and naming ceremonies

The question of how to handle the question of whether or not to have the children christened is a tricky one. The Humanist father I mentioned above reluctantly decided to let the christenings go ahead for his children, because it was so 'emotionally important' to his wife. Since the rector refused to conduct the services unless he was present, he attended them, but only on the condition that he took no active part in the proceedings himself. So he did not go forward to the font with the others, and the rector seemed satisfied with this compromise. He has, however, made it absolutely clear that he will not countenance their confirmation, until they are of an age to make an informed choice on the matter; namely, as young adults. The proposal that there should also be a Humanist naming ceremony was discussed, but it was felt that to have two ceremonies would be, 'over the top'.

Disagreements over the children

Looking at a 'mixed' marriage, admittedly from the outside, one feels it should not be too hard for two people, who love and understand each other, to cultivate tolerance over the religious issue and to respect the right of their partner to observe the practices of their belief, without criticism or resentment. But in marriages where one or both partners is very rigid in their outlook things may not go so smoothly, especially where children are involved.

Answering their questions is one thing - and as has been mentioned, children learn early that different people sometimes hold different views. It is the knowledge that your own children are being indoctrinated, (as will undoubtedly be the case in some 'mixed' marriages), that may be hard for Humanists to endure. Likewise, devoutly religious people may find it objectionable for their children to be exposed to free thinking and humanist views that they consider dangerous.

For the Humanist partner in the relationship much comfort can be derived from knowing that an overdose of religion is more than likely to act as an antidote. Another reassuring thought is that young children are unlikely to be upset if they are taken to the church or synagogue or mosque by one parent, and see the other parent taking the dog for a walk or cooking lunch. They will accept this as the norm.

If a couple has agreed in advance that religion and Humanism should be given equal status within their marriage and this is genuinely happening, it should follow naturally that both stances are given a fair hearing when issues are discussed with the children, especially when they are older. This can surely be done without any argument and, most importantly, without either parent seeking to denigrate the beliefs of the other in front of the children, either explicitly or implicitly. If this kind of attitude to differences is successfully adopted - however hard it may be for some people - this could even benefit the children in the long term by providing an object lesson in mutual respect and tolerance.

Keeping quiet

There is one further possibility that I have observed in some mixed marriages and have come across several times when involved in taking a Humanist funeral. One of the couple - and in all the cases I have known it has been the husband - seemingly makes the conscious decision not to 'rock the boat' or upset his wife over the religious issue. So he has kept his own irreligious views to himself and religion has never been discussed in the home. The children have sometimes grown up unaware that their father was a Humanist. Sometimes this has emerged after the death of the religious wife, perhaps in connection with arrangements for her funeral. A remark such as, "Of course I've never believed any of that rubbish", may surprise and shock the rest of the family. On one occasion an adult son with Humanist leanings himself came across a membership card for the Rationalist Press Association among his dead father's papers and regretted deeply that he had not known his views, in order to share them.

I cannot feel that keeping quiet in this way is the ideal solution, but perhaps it is the wisest one for some families.

Chapter ten

The extended family

The reaction of religious parents

Religious parents can be very upset when their son or daughter announces that they plan to marry a Humanist, or someone without any religious faith. In some cases they are *outraged* rather than merely *upset*. For example, to orthodox Jews or Muslims it can seem little short of catastrophic. Sadly, there are many families where the parents never become reconciled to the situation, refuse to attend the wedding and sever their relationship with the young couple.

In less extreme cases the relationship is at first under strain but later, once tempers have cooled, good sense prevails and the parties agree to differ. Often, when grandchildren arrive, the question of whether or not the child will be christened reactivates the differences and relations can become strained again if the grandparents try to exert pressure. We know there are couples who have their children christened in a religious service to keep their own parents happy, though most non-religious couples would not be happy doing this. Increasingly too, ministers are refusing to conduct such services.

Although to religious grandparents a Humanist welcoming or naming ceremony cannot but be a second best, and would possibly be resented as such, for some it can be a good compromise and help to bring opposing views together.

Tolerance from religious parents

In our family we were extremely fortunate. My husband of 42 years shed the last vestiges of religion before I met him, so I was never blamed for being an evil influence. His parents, both active members of the Church of England, welcomed me into their family and attended our Register Office wedding in a generous spirit, never expressing a hint of regret to us. It must have crossed their minds that a good, Christian daughter-in-law might have enticed their son back into the fold, but more probably they regarded his choice of a Humanist wife merely as clinching a lost cause.

More recently, many of the religious members of my husband's family have come to the Humanist wedding ceremonies of our children and have never shown anything but appreciation and pleasure. I imagine such broad mindedness and lack of resentment to be rather unusual. I think my parents-in-law tried to understand and sympathise with our Humanist viewpoint, though we never discussed it. It must have been a grief to them when their son, 'strayed from the fold', as it were. And I am grateful that they never allowed ideological differences to sour our relationship.

Interference from religious grandparents

There are some grandparents who try very hard to influence their grandchildren to make up for the absence of religion in the home. Many grandparents see a lot of the children - some even care for them when both parents are out at work - and they then have plenty of opportunity to exert influence, either overtly or subtly. There is often an extremely close bond between grandparent and grandchild.

If it becomes evident that there *is* undue influence, this presents the parents with a difficult situation. They know that their mother or father is doing what they feel to be right, yet at the same time they cannot be happy about it or allow it to go on. How they handle the matter must depend largely on what kind of relationship they have with the offending parent. If it is a close relationship where they can talk to each other freely, this will make it easier. If the relationship is more reserved or even strained, 'talking it through' will be more difficult and may cause ill feeling. But, really I see no alternative.

Other relatives

I have singled out grandparents because they are more often
closely involved in the children's upbringing, although this is less
common now families tend to be more scattered. Other relations,
or even close friends or carers, can also try to instil some religious
belief into children whom they evidently regard as deprived in
spiritual terms.

This is objectionable in exactly the same way and the child may
need protecting, unless it is happening on such a trivial scale that
it can be ignored.   In any event, whatever influence is being
brought to bear is better out in the open so that the matter can be
aired, rational decisions taken, and some satisfactory solution or
compromise found. If nothing else, the injection of some
Humanist views as an antidote can be supplied as damage
limitation.

Minimising the differences

Whatever the degree of tension there is within the extended
family on account of the religious divide, the wisest course would
seem to me to keep right away from the subject, in so far as this is
possible, just as one tries to keep off politics when views are at
different ends of the political spectrum. An exception to this
generalisation might be in families which thrive on debate, and
can discuss issues without getting too heated or upset.

There are usually so many other things that can be talked about,
from reminiscing about the past, to shared interests such as music,
food, computers, gardening or sport. Where there are young
children, these have a knack of diffusing situations and providing
a focus for adoration from both sides. Thus, by avoiding issues
that divide and concentrating on those that unite, a fairly
comfortable relationship can usually be maintained, making the
best of what can be a bad situation.

Chapter eleven

Widening horizons

Mixing with other children

I have observed that pre-school children seem to mix with others of their own age far more than was the custom some years ago when my own children were small. There are now parent and toddler groups and play groups in all but the most isolated communities. Where there is no parent at home for all or part of the working day, state nurseries, or in some cases privately run kindergartens, are where a lot of very small children first learn the hard lesson of sharing and get used to rubbing shoulders with their peers. Even where the child is in the care of a registered child minder for part of the day, there are likely to be others of a similar age.

For the parent - and it is still most usually the mother - there is also the wrench of entrusting the care of your child to other people. This severance often happens gradually, and generally only for short periods at first, but for women who go back to work a few weeks after a baby's arrival, it must be very difficult. Britain lags far behind some other European countries over maternity leave, and paternity leave is more or less unknown here. Nor do many places of employment have nursery units where mothers can be near their children during the working day and nursing mothers can feed their babies.

Other influences

As soon as one's child begins to mix with other children or be in the charge of adults from outside the immediate family, other influences will begin to come in. Many of these influences will be good and will be a valuable start to the long process of growing towards independence. Others may not be to one's liking, and parents will have to decide what to do about these.   Sometimes parents have very little choice over child care arrangements and much will depend on the facilities within reach of their home. Also, unfortunately, much may depend on what they can afford to pay.

To generalise, if parents are making a private arrangement with an individual carer, they are in a much stronger position to lay down in some detail what kind of routine they would like, even stipulating a number of do's and don'ts.   In the case of a play group or nursery, the original choice is all-important. These places do vary considerably and they are not going to alter their methods *just to please you*. Once the child has started there, it is really out of the parents' hands.   Short of removing the child if things go very wrong, there is little they can do.

Choosing a baby minder

It is natural that parents should want other adults such as child minders to use similar techniques for handling their child and to adopt the same standards of care as they do themselves. Their child's safety and physical welfare are obviously of prime importance, but there are other considerations that matter a lot, and these will vary.

For example, will the minder play, read and talk with the child, or merely put the buggy in front of the television or a video for hours on end while she gets on with her housework? Does she actually *like* children? Do they seem to like her? Does she smoke? How experienced is she at the job? How does she deal with children who are being awkward? Parents really should find out as much as they can about a potential child minder, and can ask to be put in touch with other parents who have had children looked after by her. It is better to talk with them in person than merely to have written references from them. Their ideas about what a child minder should be like and what the children should be doing all day may well be different from yours, and this can best be judged face to face.

Choosing a nursery or play group

If you do have a choice, it would seem a good idea to ask around and try to find out exactly what the options are, rather than putting your child's name down for the nearest nursery or play group. One can glean a lot about a place by talking to other parents who have children there and it is always possible to ask if one may visit perhaps for a half day while it is in action. That gives a good chance to get the feel of the place and observe whether the children are happily occupied, how they relate to each other and to the staff, and many other important details.

The religious input

In the pre-school years there can be a problem if a particular teacher or carer is pushing religion hard. Children of three and four years are extremely impressionable and will undoubtedly incorporate praying and Baby Jesus and heaven into their play and into their talk, without questioning.

How does the non-religious parent react? Calmly, I would suggest. Gently put the other point of view when the opportunity arises, without condemning any of the newly acquired religious 'belief' as *misguided rubbish*! I make some suggestions of possible ways to answer the five and six-year-old in the next chapter.

Church-based organisations

At some stage the Humanist parent will come up against a church-based group that their child wants to join. First there is Sunday School, which I can scarcely think any Humanist family would wish their child to attend, consisting, (as I imagine it does), in unadulterated Christian 'teaching'. Brownies, the junior section of Guides and Scouts, is a different matter, as there is much of value and enjoyment in their activities and, I would have thought, little harm. It did not arise in our family, as none of our children or grandchildren ever expressed a wish to join, but we would certainly not have dissuaded them. There was a branch of The Woodcraft Folk, the secular equivalent, which some of our grandchildren enjoyed for a time, but the branch sadly folded for lack of support. The Woodcraft Folk, in spite of its whimsical name, is an excellent organisation, part of the international Co-operative Movement.

For Scouts and Guides the problem is more serious. In 1990 there was a much-publicised case of a 10-year-old agnostic girl who was prevented from joining the Girl Guides because she felt unable to promise 'to do my duty to God'. While the Guides accepted girls from all *religious* backgrounds, they claimed they could not change *The Promise* to allow non-religious membership, as it was used by Guide associations throughout the world.

The case was taken up by the British Humanist Association, who discovered that there *is* an alternative Promise used in the Netherlands and elsewhere by Humanists, so this simply was not true. The BHA pointed out to the Girl Guides' Association that its manual is misleading in saying: *'Guiding for all. Because the GGA is open to all girls and women, it is important that an individual's beliefs, family culture and circumstances are respected.'* A working party was in fact set up by the GGA and it proposed a reasonable secular alternative. After prolonged discussion this was eventually rejected - and the situation is as bad as ever, so far as I know.

It seems that both for Scouts and Guides much depends on the ethos of the particular group, and whether the leader is prepared to turn a blind eye when children omit the offending sentence. One of our sons had many happy years in his Scout troop and the matter of his religious belief, (or lack of it), never arose.

Chapter twelve

Religious education

The whole issue of our children's involvement in religious education is complex and can cause Humanist parents much concern. In my view, the younger and more impressionable the child, the harder the dilemma. For the four or five-year-old, whose questions you have answered with honesty and, you hope, with openness, may now be faced with a quite different account of why things are as they are and why people act as they do. Should you exercise your legal right of withdrawal, thus inevitably making your child feel different? Or are there better ways of coping? First, one must be clear how the law stands in England and Wales at the present time.

The legal position

In the 1944 Education Act, a Daily Act of Worship and compulsory Religious Education became obligatory in maintained schools throughout England and Wales. In 1988 the Education Reform Act tightened the stranglehold of the established church still further, and it was stipulated that the Act of Worship must be 'mainly Christian'. Under both Acts parents have had the right to withdraw their child from both RE lessons and the collective Act of Worship.

Also, under the 1988 Act individual schools can apply to their local SACRE, (Standing Advisory Council for Religious Education), for a so-called 'determination', if they can show that the majority of their parents belong to one of the other world faiths. This enables them to hold assemblies in which that faith predominates. They can even apply for permission to hold multi-faith assemblies, if this is appropriate in their particular school. (This was granted in 1997 to nearly all the schools in Brent).

Overall, in England and Wales at the present time, however, very few schools have applied for determinations. Sadly, the likelihood of there being enough Humanist parents in any one school to apply for such a concession seems remote.

The early years

There are regional variations, but it is quite common for children to start school well before their fifth birthday, in some cases when they are scarcely four. Usually, they will already have attended play group or nursery for some time. These are not governed by the laws on compulsory religious education and worship. Depending largely on the personal beliefs of the staff involved, however, there can be a considerable religious input even at that early stage, which can take the Humanist parent by surprise. To a very young child what the teacher says must be true, so the religious element is taken on board along with the myriad other 'facts' that the very young assimilate with such ease. This is naturally unacceptable to the Humanist parent, and can be difficult to handle. It may be helpful to talk to the teacher, or better still the Head Teacher, and suggest that the approach to religious matters could be more balanced and open. You could express concern that your child is getting such a narrow and dogmatic view on matters which are *by no means* universally accepted. One can but try ...

As to how you should handle the situation at home is another matter. At first the child may not notice the discrepancy between what the teacher is saying and the kind of views expressed at home. But sooner or later the questions will come, and then it seems to me important to answer them fairly and not to denigrate what the teacher has been propounding. A conversation might go along these lines:

> *"Miss Higginson says that Mandy has gone to Heaven to be with Jesus".*
> *"Yes, I know that Miss Higginson thinks that, and of course Grandma believes in Heaven too. But Dad and I think rather differently, and we actually believe that when people die it is more like going to sleep, except that you don't wake up. Like when Spot died, we buried him, didn't we? We still talk about*

him and remember him, but we know that there isn't a Spot any more. When you're a bit older you can make up your own mind what you are going to think about things like that."

Should one withdraw a child?

Since 1944, parents have had the right to withdraw their children from religious assembly and from RE lessons - this is true. In reality, however, most Humanist parents do not exercise this right. There is nothing that most young children hate more than to be made to feel different. To be sent out of the classroom or to have to stand outside the hall during assembly cannot avoid *making them feel different.* There is even the risk that by isolating them in this way one is encouraging the possibility of ostracism or bullying.

If only RE were taught in an objective and balanced way and included at least some mention of Humanism, most of us would be perfectly happy for our children to take part in the lessons as a valuable aspect of their general education. If assemblies did not include worship, the same would apply. Humanist parents are truly in a dilemma. In a sense, by choosing to leave children in a religious assembly which includes worship, or at the mercy of an over enthusiastic Christian teacher, we are guilty of allowing our children to be indoctrinated. And in many instances *indoctrination* is not too strong a word, however offensive it may be to our religious friends.

The plain fact is that, at the present time, the majority of younger children come home from school with the impression that everyone believes in God. This is even the case when serious attempts to be more open are made by individual teachers. Let me give an example of this. At my five-year-old grand-daughter's infant school there is a weekly Good News Assembly at which children are praised for good work and thoughtful behaviour and given little certificates, and parents can attend. The Deputy Head who takes these assemblies, (and whom I know to be a Humanist herself), talks to the assembled children about how they can be helpful and good and hardworking, and so on. She adds, "Some of you may want to ask your god to help you." This seems to me an acceptable remark to a large group of children from a variety of religious traditions, the law being as it is.   Although it may preserve the integrity of the Humanist teacher, however, the subtlety of the wording is likely to be lost on children of that age. The same grand-daughter, Grace, a few days later, playing with friends in the garden arranged them in a circle and got them to put their hands together in prayer. So some religion is getting through!

The older child

At secondary school the question of withdrawal is rather different, as the RE lesson will not be part of an integrated day. Also, as the child gets older and grows in confidence, the question of embarrassment is less likely to arise.

It is truly ludicrous that it is the *parents* who have the right of withdrawal, even in the case of older children, but of course the wishes of your son or daughter can be the deciding factor after discussion of all the issues involved. By that age they are likely to be developing their own beliefs and views. Of our own children only one asked to be withdrawn and she later rejoined the class in the sixth form when it involved mostly discussion.

Ostracism by other children or parents

Something that should perhaps be mentioned in this chapter is the rare but unmistakable change that *can* take place in the attitude of one's children's school friends, when their parents discover that yours is a family that holds no religious beliefs. I experienced this myself when I was about 13. I had been extremely friendly at school with a girl whose elder sister was a close friend of my elder sister. We did a lot of things together and it was not until the two girls were invited to come and stay with us for part of the holiday and their parents would not allow it, that we realised why. Their father was a vicar and it became evident that he did not think that it would be a good idea for his daughters to be too much influenced by a family of infidels. At the time we were quite upset and annoyed, and the fact that my mother would certainly have allowed us to stay with *them*, had the invitation been the other way round, made the whole episode difficult for us to accept.

Educating at home

There are many reasons why some parents decide to educate their children at home. One of these, or possibly in some cases a contributory factor, may be the amount or type of religious education at the school their child would otherwise attend. In any event, home schooling gives the parent the freedom and opportunity to provide education in this whole area that is objective, fair and balanced, and to allow Humanism *alongside the religious traditions,* a status it is seldom given in schools. As we had no experience of this within our own family I have included the title of a book on home education in my reading list.

The end result

It seems to me quite impossible to find satisfactory or easy solutions for the Humanist parent with the law on RE and compulsory worship as it stands at present. We must put all our energies into fighting to change the law, so that our children are taught objectively about the main theistic and non-theistic life stances. The best way to achieve this is by joining the British Humanist Association and also your local Humanist Group, (if there is one nearby), for campaigning in your own region.

Whenever it crops up we can tell our children what our own views are on fundamental matters, while making it clear to them that others believe differently, and that it will be for them to make up their own minds when they are older. We can take comfort from the fact that the input of religion to which they are by law subjected is unlikely to do them much harm and may in fact work the other way, producing good, sceptical adults. This has certainly happened in my own family - now over four generations!

Chapter thirteen

Moral education

Morals without religion

Perhaps one of the remarks that can most irritate Humanists is when people assume that there can be no morality without religion. This view was brought home to me recently when I was taking part in a debate with a bishop in front of an invited audience at Broadcasting House on, *The Place of Religion in Society.* A Muslim gave a vivid description of how he had, personally witnessed 'a gang of Humanist vandals' running amok through the streets of Newcastle-on-Tyne! To this man, a complete absence of moral standards of behaviour was the inevitable result of an absence of religious belief. This is an extreme example, but it is a view held by many Christians that morality without religion is a contradiction in terms.

I believe them to be completely wrong and would like to suggest that Humanists may even have more highly developed moral sensibilities. They do not entrust their children's moral development and spiritual well being to the Church or to some other religious authority.

As Humanist parents we know that no religion does *not* mean no morals, but this needs stating again and again because the contrary view is always being put forward. It is taught to our children either explicitly or implicitly, and we must reassure them and show them by our own standards of behaviour that it is simply not true.

Moral teaching in the early years

It seems to me that there is far more positive reinforcement of good behaviour nowadays than there ever was in my day, from the nursery up through the infant and junior school. Encouragement, praise and reward for thoughtful or unselfish actions, and for even small improvements in children who already have behavioural problems, are all commonplace. There seems to be a greater tendency too, for teachers to draw the attention of the rest of the group to instances of good behaviour, encouraging the acquisition of moral values as a co-operative venture. Certificates and badges for being helpful or showing self control are as common as stars for good work or improvement.

Collecting my 3-year-old grandson from his nursery in Hackney recently, I was told by the teacher how proud they were of him, and I wondered what deed of heroism he had performed. Apparently it was his turn to hand round the fruit at the end of the morning, and when he got to the end of the circle there was no piece of apple left for himself, only some segments of orange which he does not like, so he had gone without. The teacher got the class to give him a round of applause for not having made a fuss!

By junior school age rewards and positive reinforcement will be rather more sophisticated, but they will still be there, side by side with sanctions when needed.

Learning from stories

One of the best ways of teaching morality is through stories. Long before children can read to themselves, story telling can play an important part in their lives, and those children who have not been lucky enough to have stories read or told to them by their parents, will certainly be able to enjoy this as soon as they start play group or nursery.

The quality of children's books seems to go from strength to strength, and even a cursory study of what is available shows that books are around in libraries, book shops and schools, which touch on all the main social and moral issues that children need to think about. Many of these books are beautifully illustrated and the stories sensitively told. There is very little religion as such, but plenty of morality, disguised as it was never disguised in Victorian children's books with their strong moral tone.

Learning from stories in the early years leads naturally to the wealth of values education that children experience in English lessons during their later school life, if the literature is well taught.

Learning by example

As well as the moral awareness that children develop as a direct result of what they learn through the school curriculum, there is the enormous influence of the school's ethos on the growing child. In my view, it is how teachers and pupils behave towards each other throughout the school day that can have almost more effect on the whole school community than anything else. Teachers sometimes underestimate the effect they are having by such things as their tone of voice, their readiness to listen to their pupils views, their fairness, their sense of humour ... Teaching is surely a terrifying responsibility - and privilege!

Good school assemblies

Another area which *can* exert positive influence is the school assembly. In our anguish over the current emphasis on Christianity, it is important to remember the number of individual teachers who are prepared to defy the Act, and do in fact conduct thoughtful and interesting assemblies where shared values within the community are explored to very good effect. This is, of course, one of the reasons why Humanist parents seldom withdraw their children, as they might then miss a valuable part of the school day. The praying and hymn singing that are usually there will probably do them little harm anyway.

Discussing moral and social issues

Nowadays at secondary school, during the years leading up to GCSE and beyond, courses in personal and social education provide a good forum for the exchange of beliefs and values, though these in no way replace English Literature as probably the best source for some of the highest quality classroom discussions on moral issues that one could hope for. These courses cover specific topics such as abortion, voluntary euthanasia, genetic engineering, human rights, racism and so on.

In this kind of lesson many teachers may welcome the presence of pupils from Humanist families, who are used to free, open and honest discussion at home. But this is not always the case and I have clear memories of feeling 'the odd one out' when such issues were discussed. As usual so much depends on the teacher in charge and I certainly remember a teacher who felt it her duty to try to put me on the 'right' path on the matter of religion.

All this can make a welcome change from RE taught with the tacit assumption that God is in charge, though there may be difficulties. The 14 or 15-year-old is likely to feel passionately that something is right or wrong, but often does not have a sufficient grasp of the arguments needed to make the case. To give an example of this feeling of frustration and impotence, my own parents were deeply involved in the fight to abolish the death penalty. Indeed, my father had worked full time for abolition and was its main protagonist in this country until his death. So, when arguments were put which I knew to be false but could not counter, I sometimes resorted (foolishly) to the words, "but *I happen to know* that ..." and this quite fairly became a joke among my friends!

Chapter fourteen

Sex education for the very young

In this country, unlike the Netherlands for example, the matter of sex education is usually left until children are eight or nine and nearing the last years at junior school. This has various disadvantages. In the first place, now that some children have already reached puberty by this age, it is far too late. Secondly, it is more than likely that much earlier they will have picked up information about sexual matters in the playground or on the street corner, from older children or contemporaries, in a 'dirty joke' sort of way. Often the information they acquire will be inaccurate or consist of half truths. If they have already been told the basic *facts of life* by their parents, this will stand them in good stead if they are with children who have been misinformed, and when they first encounter sex education at school.

Attitude to nudity

As has been referred to a number of times, children learn much from example. A completely natural and open attitude to nudity is, I suspect, usual in Humanist families, unless the parents themselves are still inhibited by their own upbringing. The feeling that there is something 'dirty' about the human body and its natural functions is 'caught not taught', and is presumably a relic of Christianity's obsessional guilt. Until recently the Catholic church went to extraordinary lengths to warn girls in particular against, 'the sins of the flesh.' Perhaps it still does in some convent schools. I shall quote two extreme examples, both of which I heard on Radio 4 recounted by people who had themselves experienced them. In one institution patent leather shoes were not allowed for fear that, when the girl went out, some unsuspecting male might glimpse a reflection of her knickers! In a second convent bananas were not allowed as their shape was considered phallic!

Honest answers

In a family where there are no feelings of shame about the human body, parents are much more likely to feel happy for their toddler to explore his or her own genitalia quite openly, as most young children will, and of course to ask all sorts of questions. They are also likely to give honest answers and not to fob their child off with some absurdity, or merely to procrastinate. When children of two or three ask where babies come from, the simple answer, "From their Mum's tummy", will be enough for the time being. If they do not ask, it may be that the question has not occurred to them and they will ask in their own good time. And when they *do* ask, I know one has to give a simple answer and restrain oneself from delivering a long lecture about everything from contraception to homosexuality. Quite often it is much later that they ask, "How do they get there?" and one can say, "Their Dad puts a seed into their Mum's tummy", or words to that effect.

Often at this age another baby is expected in the family, so 'Mum's tummy' is there for all to see, as large as life! In that situation quite detailed accounts of pregnancy and birth come very naturally, and breast feeding is accepted as the norm.

Perhaps a harder question, is "Next time you are making a baby, can I watch?" At this point it may be a good idea to explain that there are some things that people like to be private about, because they are very special. Or, 'having a quiet time on your own', may be a practice with which they are already familiar.

The mechanics of sex

The actual facts about conception and procreation are often best learned by observing the mating habits of animals, which do not mind being watched. There are, however, difficulties here. Dogs, which are most commonly seen mating by children, tend to mate roughly and greedily and children can become anxious to think that this is what goes on between their parents. I have been told by a biologist that whales and some kinds of birds mate in a much more tender way, but opportunities for observing these may be limited. One can explain that for humans, making love is a *tender* way of showing how much we care for each other.

If children end up using as it were *animal* language, it really does not matter so long as they have understood the concept. In fact a small girl I know, when asked if she knew where she came from, answered scornfully: "Of course I know - Mum and Dad *mated*!"

At some point it will be important for them to realise that sex is not only to make babies, which is a misconception that often results from the kind of partial explanation I have suggested above. But this and the importance of contraception, and indeed 'safe sex' and the risks of venereal disease, are surely not for the three-year-old!

One point to bear in mind is that other people's children may not be so well informed and their parents may be waiting to tell them in their own good time. So if one's own children, 'let the cat out of the bag', as it were, this may not go down too well. One can suggest they keep the information to themselves for the time being, rather as in the case of Father Christmas, explaining of course why.

Chapter fifteen

Gender roles

Are there genetic differences?

Among 'A' level students a preponderance of boys over girls choose mathematics as one of their subjects. Does this reflect a genetic difference in ability and character between boys and girls? Or is it purely the result of boys being encouraged to play with bricks and constructional toys when they were little? Did such play help them develop better spatial awareness than their sisters who occupied themselves with dolls' houses and nurses' outfits?

This whole subject is complex and impossible for the lay person to disentangle. But what is very clear is that there is a great deal of unfortunate conditioning and stereotyping which parents can do much to minimise. And much can be done to encourage the good qualities in children of both sexes, regardless of whether these characteristics are generally classified as male or female virtues.

Early conditioning

As soon as a baby is born and clothed, conditioning can begin. It is assumed by the traditionalists that girl babies will be dressed in pink and boy babies in blue. How else can you tell them apart? If you go against this widely accepted code, you get comments and even disapproval. Fortunately, the tradition is nowadays less universal and clothes even for the very young are obtainable in a variety of colours, including deep shades.

As children grow, however, the way they dress is very much gender-orientated, the main exception being jeans and T-shirts which are widely worn by both sexes. If parents cross the gender divide, they will certainly be criticised, especially if they allow their sons to wear anything that might be considered 'girlish'.

Equally, some toys are produced exclusively for girls, such as dolls and miniature fashion accessories, and others for boys, such as cricket bats and toy cars. I think this is very wrong. If you want boys to grow up to be good fathers and to take their full share of household chores and cooking, then surely they should be encouraged to play with dolls and shopping and cooking games as well. If you want girls to develop interests outside the home and to be as assertive as their brothers, then I see every reason to involve them in rough-and-tumble activities and mechanical toys as well as 'girlish' games.

Parental example

As ever, the way parents behave in the home is the strongest influence on the growing child. If children see that their mother does all the cooking and cleaning, while their father does the garden, decorating and DIY activities, these will be their role models. If, on the other hand, most of the cooking is done by their father and their mother paints the house and puts up shelves, then this will be their norm.

What can parents do to help children develop a wide spectrum of skills and qualities, when society expects boys to act in a certain way and girls in a different way? Any parents can try to establish within their own family a system whereby desirable male qualities are encouraged in their daughters, and desirable female qualities in their sons. It is right too that girls should expect their brothers to take an equal share in household jobs and that boys should respect their sisters' skills at woodwork and football. But what parents can achieve in this direction is severely limited in the face of the deluge of propaganda and stereotyping to which they will be subjected from other quarters.

My older daughter, who is a mother of three with a career as well and a keen feminist, admits that she found it very hard to avoid stereotyping altogether. She found herself falling into the common trap of saying to her first daughter, "You *beautiful* baby!" and then, when her son was born, " You *clever* boy!"

Some friends, who were determined that their son should not play with guns, were stymied when all the little boy's friends gathered together their discarded weapons out of pity and presented him with a positive arsenal!

Discrimination on the grounds of gender

As a Humanist I believe passionately in equal opportunities for women. Many of the religions do not, and in many parts of the world women are still treated as second class citizens. I also have feminist blood in my veins on my mother's side through three generations of women who worked for female emancipation and education. So my inbred conviction is that parents have a particular responsibility to support and encourage their daughters when they want to go into professions or undertake work where there is still discrimination against women.

There are fewer examples of situations where the discrimination is against men, but these certainly exist. Because of the nature of his freelance work, one of my sons has been able to take a very large share in the caring during the first years of his son's life. He has met remarks such as, *"Where's his mother?"* from the nurse at the welfare clinic. Other comments have taken the form of admiration and surprise. Some people have clearly shown that they do not consider him capable of taking proper care of his child. This must be a common occurrence for single fathers, as is the lack of provision for changing babies, since Mother and Baby facilities are almost always part of the women's toilets.

Chapter sixteen

The need for support

When, as a Humanist, I am asked how I can cope without the support of a god and a religion, my answer is quite simple. To religious people it may seem arrogant, but I can say with complete honesty that I feel no need for a prop of this kind. I could not with any integrity take the leap in the dark that would be necessary to acquire a religious faith, even supposing I wanted to. And as to how Humanists cope in times of trouble, we turn for emotional and practical support to our family and friends, when this is possible, and increasingly to the specialist counselling and support services which have sprung up over recent years in our society.

During the lives of most parents and children there are certainly times when support of this kind can be an enormous help, whether it is marriage difficulties, grief after the loss of a partner, disturbed behaviour in a child or other situations. It is a pity when people are too proud to seek help or admit their failure to cope on their own.

One parent families

Today there are many homes where children are being brought up by a single parent. This adult is most often the mother, but there are many lone fathers as well. Most of these parents do a wonderful job single-handed, and are often in the position they are in through no fault of their own. As well as being largely undeserved, the unpleasant generalisations made by some of our not very pleasant politicians and others about single mothers in particular are unhelpful and can only damage the children, who bear no blame.

Certainly many pregnancies are the result of ignorance, carelessness, or lack of contraceptive advice. This is an issue where Humanists would feel strongly that good sex education is of the utmost importance and is the responsibility of parents first and of schools second. The opposition of the Roman Catholic church to contraception is something that Humanists find hard to condone. The suffering and poverty in overpopulated, developing countries where Catholicism is influential, are largely the result of this teaching. Contraception is always better than abortion. But, when contraception has not been used or has failed, the early termination of unwanted pregnancies would seem to me - and probably to most Humanists - to be the best solution, if this is what the parents, (or sometimes only the mother), decide to choose.

But far more often women, and less frequently men, are left to bring up children on their own as the result of death, separation or divorce. Sometimes the father leaves the scene even before the baby's birth. Unless or until the single parent finds a new partner or remarries, single parents have to cope on their own. It is bound to be hard, and much depends on the ages of the children, the support that is available and the financial circumstances of the family.

My own father died when I was four months old and my mother never remarried. My sisters and I were brought up by my mother and her elder sister. She virtually gave up her own career as a doctor to help with our upbringing, and she provided additional love and support throughout our childhood and beyond. I did not appreciate the extent of her sacrifice until many years later, and I would think it was quite unusual. In earlier generations unmarried aunts and sisters often stepped in when mothers died in childbirth, but fortunately this is now a rare occurrence.

Practical support for the single parent has been slow in coming, but at last their predicament is being recognised by the government. Provision is starting to be made to help them out of the so-called 'poverty trap' and into work, when this is appropriate and when adequate arrangements for child care can be arranged.

Separation and divorce

With over one third of marriages now ending in divorce in this country, it is becoming increasingly rare to find neither in an extended family. But this is currently the case in ours so I cannot speak from first hand experience. I *have,* however, been involved with developing Humanist wedding ceremonies, and three of our children had Humanist weddings. So I do know the importance Humanists put on the commitment and responsibility that are involved in marriage and long term relationships. The view sometimes voiced - that their commitment cannot be a serious one since they do not make vows before 'God' - is quite untrue. The words used by Humanist couples to express their aspirations and ideals are most moving - and they are chosen by each individual couple to state their commitment to each other and their vision of their life together.

Where the marriage does break down, a Humanist couple will suffer as much distress as a religious couple. But our sense of failure and probably guilt will come from the hurt we have inflicted and suffered, and the fact that we have not been able to fulfil our aspirations and ideals. It will not come from our failure to honour vows we made before 'God'.

Parents are now aware of the long term damage that their splitting up is likely to inflict on their children. And however much, as a Humanist, one may welcome humane divorce law and abhor the idea of couples having to stay together when the relationship has broken down utterly, this knowledge must be a cause of immense grief and concern. Remarriage can bring normality into the family again, but step-families demand huge adjustment and under-standing, both from the children and the adults involved.

Bereavement and other counselling

I was shocked to hear a figure quoted on the radio the other day. It was based on a substantial bit of research which claimed that *one third* of children in an average class at school in the UK today are grieving.

This grief was generally as a result of losing a parent at some time in their lives, not necessarily recently, and manifested itself in many different ways; in their behaviour, their progress at school and their general well being. The loss was presumably caused by the split up of their parents, more often than by death.

Counselling and therapy are nowadays widely available both for parents and children. Some schools even employ professional counsellors to help their pastoral staff, who usually have neither the time nor the expertise to handle the needs of grieving or disturbed children.

If children have never known the missing parent, as in my own case, they accept their one parent as the norm to begin with. It is later that it can hit you that you have not a father like other children. I remember going through a bad patch when I was eleven, and grieving by myself about the father I never had. It was at this time, too, that I refused to go to school. Counselling would have helped me, I feel sure.

Chapter seventeen

Towards independence

I wonder how many parents can honestly say that the period when
their children were adolescents was as easy and happy as when
they were younger. How many, with hindsight, wish they had
acted differently? Certainly some young people pass through this
stage of growing up much more smoothly than others, so is this
merely a matter of luck? Or, if things *do* become difficult, should
parents blame themselves for having mishandled things? To what
extent are such problems the direct result of there being a poor
relationship between parent and child dating back many years,
perhaps with an absence of mutual trust and affection? Or is
there simply an obstinate streak in your child which has always
been there but has now blossomed?

Fortunately, the worries and the problems which at times can
threaten to engulf parents do, in the vast majority of cases,
subside, whatever ideas to the contrary one may glean from the
media. So the question is how to weather the storm while it lasts.

Rebellion

In a book of this kind that is to a large extent anecdotal, I have no
intention of recounting episodes from the adolescent years of our
own four children, for their sake. This is a shame because in
retrospect some of them were quite funny. I will, however, admit
that it was over the issue of smoking that we ran into trouble. I
had never tried to conceal my dislike of the habit and had stressed
the health hazards - although at that time the extent of these was
not fully known. According to one of my daughters, I over-
stressed the dangers, and she says she was relieved to discover
later that every single person who smokes does not automatically
die of lung cancer!

The result, of course, was that two of them had become quite heavy smokers before we found out - the two, as it happened who had suffered from childhood asthma. It caused me a lot of misery at the time, and I am happy to report that they both gave up smoking as adults. But in retrospect I have no doubt at all that I caused this by my attitude. In other areas, where we were liberal and tolerant, there was not the same opportunity for rebellion.

Looking further back to my own teenage years, I followed a similar pattern and was rebellious and difficult at school when the rules did not suit me, but not at home where there was no particular cause for disagreement. Often it is the other way round.

Growing freedom

The process of growing towards independence that begins when children start school or before, moves on rapidly during the adolescent years and can cause concern. Many parents find it difficult to adjust to treating their children as adults, and letting them make their own mistakes. If they have been allowed to enjoy a certain amount of freedom from an early age, then this transition to greater independence will come more easily.

In many families it will be the well established norm at this stage for rules and limits to be agreed after discussion and negotiation - over contentious issues such as when children should come home after going out in the evening. It helps a lot if they are used to this way of reaching consensus. If, on the other hand, the child has been brought up in the, 'because I say so' school, then, in my view, there is bound to be trouble when freedom beckons.

At this age, as when the children were younger, it is reasonable for parents to know where they are and when to expect them home. If their plans change, it is reasonable that they should ring to let their parents know. This is a matter of being considerate which parents surely have a right to expect. In return, the young people want above all to be trusted. What is crucial is to keep lines of communication open between both parties, however tenuous these may seem at times.

The real dangers

As young people become more independent and start to lead lives of their own, so parents inevitably have less control over what they are doing. This is obvious. It is also obvious that there are potential dangers and pitfalls out there, even though these are sometimes exaggerated by the media. And, however much one may wish to think well of the human race, there are certainly some unpleasant, unscrupulous and violent people around. So, apart from worrying themselves sick, (which does not help anyone much), what can parents do to protect their young?

First, I think one should draw a distinction between dangers about which parents can do very little, and others for which parents can and should prepare their children. The first category might include unprovoked violence or those accidents which are not uncommon in high risk sports. The second much more common type of danger would include alcohol and drugs, unprotected sex, taking lifts from strangers, involvement with strange cults and so on. It is in this latter category where I would suggest that the kind of approach practised in many Humanist families can help.

An accurate knowledge of the facts and free and informed discussion are surely the best protection against these genuine dangers, some of which young people may have had to cope with before they have even reached their teens. Many schools now have visiting experts who come into the class as outsiders and as such are better able to handle some of these sensitive and crucially important issues, as well as being trained to do so. Using imaginative techniques, much effective work is done with children, many of whom are totally ignorant or grossly misinformed.

Input from people nearer their own age is always valuable, for we all know that dire warnings from older people usually have little effect. At home, meal times around the family table with older siblings taking part, can provide an excellent forum for the exchange of experience and information.

Leaving the nest

Adolescence is a time when much tolerance and understanding may be called for from parents. But when these years of transition and change have been weathered, a new relationship will have emerged between parent and child. The birds may have left the nest but, hopefully, they will choose to return again and again, and will always be welcome.

Further information

HUMANISM is a way of living which relies on human beings and the natural world. Humanists are atheists in the sense that they live their lives without reference to a god or any supernatural force and, more importantly, they find in human nature a rational basis for morality. *Morals Without Religion,* is probably the phrase that best sums up what Humanism is about.

Since Humanists believe that this world is the only one they expect to experience, they are well motivated to make it a better and happier place now, and for generations yet unborn. There are Humanist organisations all over the world working to promote scientific enquiry and freedom of belief, and to combat superstition, persecution and intolerance.

Happy family life and warm human relationships are central to Humanism, and it is in their own and other people's children that Humanists find their version of immortality.

* * * * * * *

Free leaflets and further information about Humanism can be obtained from:

The British Humanist Association
47 Theobald's Road
London WC1X 8SP

Telephone: 0171 430 0908

A publications list can be obtained from the Rationalist Press Association at the same address.

The British Humanist Association also publishes the three ceremony booklets mentioned:

New Arrivals,
Sharing The Future, and
Funerals Without God.

These are practical guidelines to non-religious baby naming, wedding and funeral ceremonies. The first of these titles can be bought from the British Humanist Association for £3-50; the other two cost £5-00. Postage is included.

Home-based education or 'home-schooling'

For information about home schooling, which is mentioned as an option in Chapter 12, Roland Meighan's book, *The Next Learning System: and why home-schoolers are trailblazers,* is recommended. This can be bought from Educational Heretics Press, 113 Arundel Drive, Bramcote Hills, Nottingham NG9 3FQ for £7·95, postage included.

An information pack published by Education Now costs £10·00, postage included, and a video *The Family Strikes Back: a video introduction to the home-based education alternative to schooling,* costs £15·00, postage included, and both are available from the same address.

The photographs show the children of Jane and William Wynne Willson at two different stages in their lives.